Th. Jefferson
Booker T. Washington
Henry Ford
Paul "Bear" Bryant
Theodore Roosevelt
Harry Truman
Albert Einstein
Th. Jefferson
Dale Carnegie
Theodore Roosevelt
Albert Schweitzer
Vince Lombardi
G. Washington
Martin Luther King, Jr.
Abraham Lincoln
G. S. Patton, Jr.
Ray Kroc
Harry Truman
Dwight D. Eisenhower
Golda Meir
Dwight D. Eisenhower
Franklin D. Roosevelt
Andrew Jackson
B. Franklin
Paul "Bear" Bryant
Joannes Paulus PP. II
Booker T. Washington
Douglas MacArthur
Abraham Lincoln
Douglas MacArthur
M K Gandhi
Walt Disney
Mother Teresa
Dwight D. Eisenhower
C. de Gaulle
Harry Truman
Norman Vincent Peale
Franklin D. Roosevelt
Henry Ford
Helen Keller
G. Washington
Booker T. Washington
Vince Lombardi
John Wooden
M K Gandhi
C. de Gaulle
Dale Carnegie
Andrew Jackson
Albert Einstein
Joannes Paulus PP. II
Golda Meir
Golda Meir
B. Franklin
Winston Churchill
Paul "Bear" Bryant
Henry Ford
Walt Disney
M K Gandhi
Dale Carnegie
Walt Disney

Booker T. Washington
Henry Ford
Paul "Bear" Bryant
Theodore Roosevelt
Harry Truman
Albert Einstein
Dale Carnegie
Albert Schweitzer
Vince Lombardi
G. Washington
Martin Luther King, Jr.
Abraham Lincoln
G. S. Patton, Jr.
Harry Truman
Dwight D. Eisenhower
Golda Meir
Dwight D. Eisenhower
Franklin D. Roosevelt
Andrew Jackson
B. Franklin
"Bear" Bryant
Joannes Paulus PP. II
Booker T. Washington
Abraham Lincoln
Douglas MacArthur
M. K. Gandhi
Walt Disney
Harry Truman
Norman Vincent Peale
Franklin D. Roosevelt
Henry Ford
G. Washington
Booker T. Washington
Helen Keller
Vince Lombardi
John Wooden
M. K. Gandhi
C. de Gaulle
Dale Carnegie
Andrew Jackson
Albert Einstein
Joannes Paulus PP. II
Golda Meir
Golda Meir
B. Franklin
Paul "Bear" Bryant
Henry Ford
Walt Disney
M. K. Gandhi
Walt Disney

GREAT QUOTES FROM GREAT LEADERS

GREAT QUOTES FROM GREAT LEADERS

COMPILED BY PEGGY ANDERSON · ILLUSTRATED BY MICHAEL MCKEE

CELEBRATING EXCELLENCE PUBLISHING

We are grateful to Encyclopaedia Britannica, Inc. for permission to reprint its copyrighted materials and use the 15th edition as the primary source for biographical information.

Authentic signatures not available for Aristotle, Confucius and Lech Walesa at the time of publication.

GREAT QUOTES FROM GREAT LEADERS compiled by Peggy Anderson

Book design & illustrations by Michael McKee

 For information, write Celebrating Excellence Publishing, 919 Springer Drive, Lombard, Illinois 60148-6416. Telephone (708) 953-8440.

ISBN: 1-880461-02-1

9 Printing/AK/Year 95 94 93

TABLE OF CONTENTS

"He who learns of all men is wise."

— Anonymous

Dedicated in
loving memory to
my father.

PREFACE

Great Leaders come from diverse backgrounds — writers, philosophers, sports figures, business magnates, politicians and scientists. Some lived very humble lives, while others constantly were subjected to the scrutiny of the public eye. Many had amassed great fortunes, while others lived in poverty. All had intrinsic wealth derived from personal achievement and commitment to a worthy cause.

The common thread that binds them together is leadership. The drive and devotion that they brought to their specific fields of endeavor inspired countless others to reach for life's greatest achievements. They were true pioneers, teaching others not only through their actions, but through their words.

Brought together in this volume are some of those inspiring words to captivate the hearts and minds of present and future generations.

Sir Winston Churchill — author, orator, and statesman — led Great Britain from the brink of defeat to victory as wartime prime minister. Born in Oxfordshire, England in 1874, Churchill began serving his country as a military leader in World War I. As a member of Parliament, his repeated warnings of the menace of Hitler's Germany, combined with his aggressive and convincing oratory skills, resulted in his appointment to prime minister in 1939.

He joined Franklin D. Roosevelt and Joseph Stalin in 1940 to shape Allied strategy in World War II. An intense patriot and romantic believer in his country's greatness, Churchill gave his people the strong leadership and devotion that ultimately led to Britain's military salvation.

He was awarded the Nobel Peace Prize for literature in 1953 for his book, *The Second World War,* and also was knighted the same year.

WINSTON CHURCHILL

The price of greatness is responsibility.

The greatest lesson in life is to know that even fools are right sometimes.

Personally, I'm always ready to learn, although I do not always like being taught.

Some men change their party for the sake of their principles; others their principles for the sake of their party.

It was the nation and the race dwelling all round the globe that had the lion's heart. I had the luck to be called upon to give the roar.

He has all the virtues I dislike and none of the vices I admire.

Winston S. Churchill

An appeaser is one who feeds a crocodile, hoping it will eat him last.

Eating words has never given me indigestion.

Nothing is more costly, nothing is more sterile, than vengeance.

Without courage, all other virtues lose their meaning.

To gain one's way is no escape from the responsibility for an inferior solution.

Politics are almost as exciting as war, and quite as dangerous. In war you can only be killed once, but in politics many times.

Winston S. Churchill

We do not covet anything from any nation except their respect.

A fanatic is one who can't change his mind and won't change the subject.

There is no finer investment for any community than putting milk into babies.

It is a mistake to look too far ahead. Only one link in the chain of destiny can be handled at a time.

Moral of the Work. In war: resolution. In defeat: defiance. In victory: magnanimity. In peace: goodwill.

Winston S. Churchill

Soldier, statesman, writer and explorer, Theodore Roosevelt became the 26th President of the United States. His enormous energy and zest for life made him one of America's most flamboyant leaders.

Roosevelt served as assistant secretary of the Navy before resigning in 1898 to fight in Cuba. Returning as something of a war hero, he easily was elected governor of New York. He then served as Vice President of the United States and took office after McKinley's assassination in 1901.

Roosevelt greatly expanded the powers of the presidency and of the federal government on the side of public interest in conflicts between big business and big labor. He won the Nobel Peace Prize in 1906 for mediating the end of the Russo-Japanese War and promoted the construction of the Panama Canal. A devout naturalist, Roosevelt was responsible for setting aside thousands of acres of land to preserve what is today our national parks and forests.

THEODORE ROOSEVELT

Theodore Roosevelt

The credit belongs to the man who is actually in the arena; whose face is marred by dust and sweat and blood; who strives valiantly; who errs and comes short again and again; who knows the great enthusiasms, the great devotions, and spends himself in a worthy cause; who at the best knows in the end the triumph of high achievement; and who at the worst, if he fails, at least fails while daring greatly. . .

No man is above the law and no man below it.

Speak softly and carry a big stick; you will go far.

Far and away the best prize that life offers is the chance to work hard at work worth doing.

Theodore Roosevelt

O bedience of the law is demanded; not asked as a favor.

The best executive is the one who has sense enough to pick good men to do what he wants done, and self-restraint enough to keep from meddling with them while they do it.

In any moment of decision the best thing you can do is the right thing, the next best thing is the wrong thing, and the worst thing you can do is nothing.

Don't spread patriotism too thin.

Aggressive fighting for the right is the greatest sport in the world.

Theodore Roosevelt

Don't foul, don't flinch — hit the line hard.

Nine-tenths of wisdom consists in being wise in time.

Get action. Seize the moment. Man was never intended to become an oyster.

I think there is only one quality worse than hardness of heart and that is softness of head.

No man is justified in doing evil on the ground of expediency.

No man is worth his salt who is not ready at all times to risk his body, to risk his well-being, to risk his life, in a great cause.

Theodore Roosevelt

Martin Luther King, Jr. used his strong personality and eloquent oratory to spearhead the civil rights movement in the United States during the 1950s and 1960s. A Baptist minister, King began his civil rights activities in 1955 with the successful boycott of the segregated bus system in Montgomery, Alabama.

He founded the Southern Christian Leadership Conference in 1957 in an effort to mobilize the nonviolent struggle against racism and discrimination. On August 28, 1963, the massive "March on Washington" culminated in 200,000 Americans of all races gathering at the Lincoln Memorial to hear King speak.

The movement won a major victory in 1964 when Congress passed the Civil Rights Act, and King became the youngest man ever to receive the Nobel Peace Prize. The world lost a towering symbol of liberty and justice when an assassin's bullet claimed his life in 1968.

MARTIN LUTHER KING, JR.

Martin Luther King, Jr.

I have a dream that one day this nation will rise up and live out the true meaning of this creed—We hold these truths to be self-evident: that all men are created equal . . .

Darkness cannot drive out darkness; only light can do that. Hate cannot drive out hate; only love can do that.

Injustice anywhere is a threat to justice everywhere.

If a man is called to be a streetsweeper, he should sweep streets even as Michelangelo painted or Beethoven composed music or Shakespeare wrote poetry. He should sweep streets so well that all the hosts of heaven and earth will pause to say, ''Here lived a great streetsweeper who did his job well.''

Nothing pains some people more than having to think.

Martin Luther King, Jr.

I believe that unarmed truth and unconditional love will have the final word in reality.

We must use time creatively — and forever realize that the time is always hope to do great things.

We must combine the toughness of the serpent and the softness of the dove, a tough mind and a tender heart.

Man is man because he is free to operate within the framework of his destiny. He is free to deliberate, to make decisions, and to choose between alternatives.

Man must evolve for all human conflict a method which rejects revenge, aggression and retaliation. The foundation of such a method is love.

Martin Luther King, Jr.

If a man hasn't discovered something that he will die for, he isn't fit to live.

We must develop and maintain the capacity to forgive. He who is devoid of the power to forgive is devoid of the power to love.

When evil men plot, good men must plan. When evil men shout ugly words of hatred, good men must commit themselves to the glories of love.

When we let freedom ring, when we let it ring from every village and every hamlet, from every state and every city, we will be able to speed up that day when all of God's children, black men and white men, Jews and Gentiles, Protestants and Catholics, will be able to join hands and sing in the words of that old Negro spiritual, ''Free at last! Free at last! Thank God Almighty, we are free at last!''

Martin Luther King, Jr.

Professional football coach Vince Lombardi became a national symbol of single-minded determination to win. In nine seasons as the head coach of the previously moribund Green Bay Packers, Lombardi led the team to five NFL championships and to victory in the first two Super Bowls.

At Fordham University, Lombardi played guard on the famous line known as the "Seven Blocks of Granite." He studied law at Fordham and had a brief career as a minor league football player before becoming a high school coach in 1939. After serving as an assistant coach in college and in the pros, he was hired as head coach and general manager of the Green Bay Packers in 1959. His Spartan training regimen and personal drive turned the Green Bay Packers from a team accustomed to defeat to the paragon of victory.

He went on to become head coach, general manager and part owner of the Washington Redskins before dying of cancer in 1970.

VINCE LOMBARDI

Vince Lombardi

The quality of a person's life is in direct proportion to their commitment to excellence, regardless of their chosen field of endeavor.

It's not whether you get knocked down, it's whether you get up.

The difference between a successful person and others is not a lack of strength, not a lack of knowledge, but rather in a lack of will.

The harder you work, the harder it is to surrender.

Winning is a habit. Unfortunately, so is losing.

Vince Lombardi

The spirit, the will to win, and the will to excel are the things that endure. These qualities are so much more important than the events that occur.

In great attempts it is glorious even to fail.

Football is like life — it requires perseverance, self-denial, hard work, sacrifice, dedication and respect for authority.

Build for your team a feeling of oneness, of dependence upon one another and of strength to be derived by unity.

I firmly believe that any man's finest hour — his greatest fulfillment to all he holds dear — is that moment when he has worked his heart out in a good cause and lies exhausted on the field of battle — victorious.

Vince Lombardi

Winning is not a sometime thing; it's an all-the-time thing.

It is and always has been an American seal to be first in anything we do and to win and to win and to win.

If you can accept losing, you can't win.

Winning is not everything — but making the effort to win is.

We know how rough the road will be, how heavy here the load will be, we know about the barricades that wait along the track, but we have set our soul ahead upon a certain goal ahead and nothing left from hell to sky shall ever turn us back.

Vince Lombardi

Golda Meir was a founder of the State of Israel and served as its fourth prime minister (1969-74). Born in Kiev, the Ukraine, in 1898, she emigrated to Wisconsin in 1906. Her political activity began as a leader in the Milwaukee Labor Zionist Party.

After emigrating to Palestine in 1921, she held key posts in the Jewish Agency and in the World Zionist Organization. After Israel proclaimed its independence in 1948, she served as minister of labor and then foreign minister. She was appointed prime minister in 1969.

During her administration, she worked for a peace settlement in the Middle East using diplomatic means. Her efforts at forging peace were halted by the outbreak of the fourth Arab-Israeli War. She resigned her post in 1974 but remained an important political figure throughout her retirement. Her true strength and spirit were emphasized when, after her death in 1978, it was revealed that she had suffered from leukemia for 12 years.

G O L D A   M E I R

Golda Meir

Those who do not know how to weep with their whole heart don't know how to laugh either.

You cannot shake hands with a clenched fist.

I can honestly say that I was never affected by the question of the success of an undertaking. If I felt it was the right thing to do, I was for it regardless of the possible outcome.

Old age is like a plane flying through a storm. Once you're aboard, there's nothing you can do.

A leader who doesn't hesitate before he sends his nation into battle is not fit to be a leader.

Golda Meir

The 16th President of the United States, Abraham Lincoln preserved the Union during the American Civil War. Lincoln's inner qualities of faithfulness, honesty, resolution, humor and courage gave him the strength to lead his country during the bloodiest years of its existence.

Born in the backwoods of Kentucky in 1809, Lincoln worked as a rail splitter, flatboatman, storekeeper, postmaster and surveyor before becoming a lawyer. His debates while running for the Senate made him a nationally known figure, and he was elected President in 1860.

By the time Lincoln had taken office, seven states already had seceded from the Union over the issue of slavery. Lincoln issued his Emancipation Proclamation in 1863 to set the slaves in the rebellious states free. He coordinated every aspect of the war effort as commander-in-chief, and his military genius was instrumental in the Union victory. Re-elected in 1864, Lincoln tragically was assassinated before he could oversee the Reconstruction of the South.

ABRAHAM LINCOLN

Abraham Lincoln

Nearly all men can stand adversity, but if you want to test a man's character, give him power.

A drop of honey catches more flies than a gallon of gall. So with men. If you would win a man to your cause, first convince him that you are his sincere friend. Therein is a drop of honey which catches his heart, which, say what he will, is the highroad to his reason.

The best thing about the future is that it comes only one day at a time.

What kills a skunk is the publicity it gives itself.

Tact: the ability to describe others as they see themselves.

Abraham Lincoln

It has been my experience that folks who have no vices have very few virtues.

No man has a good enough memory to make a successful liar.

When you have got an elephant by the hind legs and he is trying to run away, it's best to let him run.

I don't think much of a man who is not wiser today than he was yesterday.

I will prepare and some day my chance will come.

Am I not destroying my enemies when I make friends of them?

Abraham Lincoln

Always bear in mind that your own resolution to succeed is more important than any other one thing.

I do the very best I know how — the very best I can; and I mean to keep on doing so until the end.

Force is all-conquering, but its victories are short-lived.

You cannot help men permanently by doing for them what they could and should do for themselves.

My dream is of a place and a time where America will once again be seen as the last best hope of earth.

Abraham Lincoln

The upbeat religious philosophy and oratorical skill of Norman Vincent Peale made him one of the most popular Protestant ministers in the United States. He utilized the mass media — radio, television and the newspapers — to bring his message on the benefits of prayer to millions of people.

The son of a Methodist preacher from Bowersville, Ohio, Peale graduated from Ohio Wesleyan University in 1920. He attended Boston University School of Theology, and was ordained by the Methodist Church in 1922. Ten years later, Peale was named minister of the Marble Collegiate Reformed Church in New York. Believing that one of the main tasks of religion is to help people, Peale wrote several books on the subject, including *The Power of Positive Thinking.*

His buoyant faith in God and his belief in the power of prayer and positive thinking were the cornerstones of his message. Peale also helped found the American Foundation of Religion and Psychiatry.

NORMAN VINCENT PEALE

Norman Vincent Peale

Any fact facing us is not as important as our attitude toward it, for that determines our success or failure.

It is a fact that you project what you are.

The trouble with most of us is that we would rather be ruined by praise than saved by criticism.

Believe you are defeated, believe it long enough, and it is likely to become a fact.

Plan your work for today and every day, then work your plan.

Think enthusiastically about everything; but especially about your job. If you do so, you'll put a touch of glory in your life. If you love your job with enthusiasm, you'll shake it to pieces.

Norman Vincent Peale

Never mention the worst. Never think of it. Drop it out of your consciousness.

I expect the best and with God's help will attain the best.

When every physicial and mental resource is focused, one's power to solve a problem multiplies tremendously.

Become a possibilitarian. No matter how dark things seem to be or actually are, raise your sights and see possibilities — always see them, for they're always there.

We tend to get what we expect.

We struggle with the complexities and avoid the simplicities.

Norman Vincent Peale

Think positively about yourself, keep your thoughts and your actions clean, ask God who made you to keep on remaking you.

Americans are so tense and keyed up that it is impossible even to put them to sleep with a sermon.

Every problem has in it the seeds of its own solution. If you don't have any problems, you don't get any seeds.

When you affirm big, believe big, and pray big, big things happen.

People must be taught to realize that in faith they have a mechanism and power by which they can actually live victorious, happy, and successful lives.

Norman Vincent Peale

As founder of the McDonald's Corporation, Ray A. Kroc largely is responsible for revolutionizing the restaurant industry. His persistence, diligence and faithfulness set the standard for modern business leadership.

Kroc's opportunity for success came in the form of a small restaurant in San Bernardino, California, run by the McDonald brothers. Their assembly-line method of serving hamburgers, french fries and milk shakes was simple but efficient. Kroc knew that this concept would have a great appeal to consumers.

The first of Kroc's McDonald's was opened April 15, 1955. Kroc continued to expand by introducing a unique franchise system. His methods and ideas about customer service have served as models for many different industries.

Kroc's steadfast devotion to an idea brought him personal success, and also allowed him to set up several charities and educational organizations.

RAY KROC

The quality of an individual is reflected in the standards they set for themselves.

It's a matter of having principles. It's easy to have principles when you're rich. The important thing is to have principles when you're poor.

When you're green, you're growing; and when you're ripe, you start to rot.

What we have created is a business organization dedicated to rigid principles.

You're only as good as the people you hire.

Albert Schweitzer, who has been called one of the greatest Christians of his time, was a brilliant philosopher, musician, theologian and physician.

Schweitzer was born in 1875 in the region of Alsace, Germany. At the age of 21, he decided to devote the next nine years of his life to science, music and preaching. By the time he was 30, he had an international reputation as a writer on theology, a gifted organist, and an authority on the life and works of Johann Sebastian Bach.

While principal of St. Thomas Theological College, he became inspired to become a medical missionary. After studying medicine and surgery for six years, he built his own hospital in Africa. Schweitzer used the proceeds from his concerts and lectures to equip and maintain the hospital. He later set up a leper colony.

Public acknowledgement of his selfless commitment to humanity was bestowed upon him in 1952, when he won the Nobel Peace Prize.

ALBERT SCHWEITZER

Albert Schweitzer

Example is not the main thing in influencing others. It is the only thing.

One truth stands firm. All that happens in world history rests on something spiritual. If the spiritual is strong, it creates world history. If it is weak, it suffers world history.

There is no higher religion than human service. To work for the common good is the greatest creed.

Man must cease attributing his problems to his environment, and learn again to exercise his will — his personal responsibility.

To affirm life is to deepen, and to exalt the will to live.

Albert Schweitzer

Do something for somebody every day for which you do not get paid.

We must all die. But that I can save him from days of torture, that is what I feel as my great and ever new privilege.

Whosoever is spared personal pain must feel himself called to help in diminishing the pain of others.

The purpose of human life is to serve, and to show compassion and the will to help others.

Do not let Sunday be taken from you...If your soul has no Sunday, it becomes an orphan.

Albert Schweitzer

I don't know what your destiny will be, but one thing I know: the only ones among you who will be really happy are those who will have sought and found how to serve.

An optimist is a person who sees a green light everywhere, while the pessimist sees only the red stoplight. . . .The truly wise person is colorblind.

Reverence for life is the highest court of appeal.

A man is ethical only when life, as such, is sacred to him.

Truth has no special time of its own. Its hour is now — always.

Albert Schweitzer

The third President of the United States and its first secretary of state, Thomas Jefferson is best remembered as the principal author of the Declaration of Independence.

A wealthy Virginia planter, Jefferson began his political career as a member of the House of Burgesses in 1769. Later, as a delegate to the Second Continental Congress, he was appointed along with Benjamin Franklin and John Adams to draft a formal statement of reasons for separation from Great Britain. The resultant Declaration of Independence, largely penned by Jefferson, summed up the commitment of the young country to life, liberty and self-government.

He went on to serve as the U.S. minister in France before accepting George Washington's appointment as the first secretary of state. Assuming the Presidency in 1801, he soon doubled the size of the United States with the purchase of the Louisiana Territory from Napoleon. He devoted his life in retirement to establishing the University of Virginia.

THOMAS JEFFERSON

Th: Jefferson

We hold these truths to be self-evident: That all men are created equal; that they are endowed by their Creator with certain unalienable rights; that among these are life, liberty, and the pursuit of happiness. . .

The God who gave us life, gave us liberty at the same time.

No man will ever bring out of the Presidency the reputation which carries him into it.

It is the trade of lawyers to question everything, yield nothing, and talk by the hour.

Eternal vigilance is the price of liberty.

Th: Jefferson

The most valuable of all talents is that of never using two words when one will do.

He who permits himself to tell a lie once, finds it much easier to do it a second time.

We confide in our strength, without boasting of it; we respect that of others, without fearing it.

The care of human life and happiness, and not their destruction, is the first and only legitimate object of good government.

When angry, count ten before you speak; if very angry, one hundred.

A mind always employed is always happy. This is the true secret, the grand recipe, for felicity.

Honesty is the first chapter of the book of wisdom.

I'm a great believer in luck, and I find the harder I work the more I have of it.

Never trouble another for what you can do for yourself.

Whenever you are to do a thing, though it can never be known but to yourself, ask yourself how you would act were all the world looking at you, and act accordingly.

Th: Jefferson

Andrew Carnegie stands as the embodiment of entrepreneurial success and civic responsibility. He believed in hard work and put that belief into motion at an early age. He came to America with his family from Scotland in 1848, and started work at age 13 as a bobbin boy in a cotton factory for $1.25 a week. Carnegie never stopped working and soon moved on to the telegraph office for the railroad.

Recognizing the needs of the growing railroad industry, Carnegie borrowed money and invested his small salary in both oil and steel. The return on these investments would culminate in the formation of the mammoth Carnegie Steel Company.

The sale of his steel company made Carnegie one of the wealthiest individuals of his time. He used his huge fortune to lead the way in establishing many cultural, educational and scientific institutions. The Carnegie Corporation, founded in 1911, sponsored the creation of thousands of public libraries throughout the world.

ANDREW CARNEGIE

As I grow older I pay less attention to what men say. I just watch what they do.

There is no use whatever trying to help people who do not help themselves. You cannot push anyone up a ladder unless he is willing to climb himself.

Concentration is my motto — first honesty, then industry, then concentration.

The law of competition is best for the race, because it insures survival of the fittest.

All honor's wounds are self-inflicted.

Andrew Carnegie

Surplus wealth is a sacred trust which its possessor is bound to administer in his lifetime for the good of the community.

On partnership: ''Mr. Morgan buys his partners; I grow my own.''

Concentration: put all your eggs in one basket, and watch that basket.

We know that man was created, not with an instinct for his own degradation, but imbued with the desire and the power for improvement to which, perchance, there may be no limit short of perfection even here in this life upon earth.

The first man gets the oyster, the second man gets the shell.

Andrew Carnegie

The average person puts only 25% of his energy and ability into his work. The world takes off its hat to those who put in more than 50% of their capacity, and stands on its head for those few and far between souls who devote 100%.

Aim for the highest.

The man who acquires the ability to take full possession of his own mind may take possession of anything else to which he is justly entitled.

I believe that the true road to preeminent success in any line is to make yourself master of that line.

The ties of brotherhood still bind together the rich and poor in harmonious relationships.

Andrew Carnegie

Legendary football coach Knute Rockne built the University of Notre Dame into a major power in college football. The success of his teams and his humorous, colorful personality captured the public's imagination during the "golden age" of American sports in the 1920s.

Born in Voss, Norway, Rockne came to the United States with his family in 1893. He attended the University of Notre Dame as a chemistry student, where he also ran track and played end on the football team. He graduated with honors in 1914, but remained at the university as a chemistry instructor and assistant football coach. He became head coach and athletic director in 1918.

In 13 seasons, Rockne's "Fighting Irish" won 105 games while losing only 12 and tying 5. He coached his teams to three national championships and five undefeated seasons. Rockne was a brilliant strategist and a tremendous motivator. His winning percentage of .881 is the highest in college football history.

KNUTE ROCKNE

Knute Rockne

An automobile goes nowhere efficiently unless it has a quick, hot spark to ignite things, to set the cogs of the machine in motion. So I try to make every player on my team feel he's the spark keeping our machine in motion. On him depends our successes.

Show me a good and gracious loser and I'll show you a failure.

One loss is good for the soul. Too many losses are not good for the coach.

I won't know why we lost the game until my barber tells me on Monday.

One man practicing sportsmanship is far better than a hundred teaching it.

Knute Rockne

American printer, publisher, author, inventor, scientist and diplomat, Benjamin Franklin is best remembered for his role in separating the American colonies from Great Britain and in helping to frame the Declaration of Independence.

Franklin continued his efforts as an inventor and scientist throughout his diplomatic career, inventing the Franklin stove, bifocal spectacles and the lightning rod. He was the first to institute such public services as a fire department, a lending library, and a learning academy, which later became the University of Pennsylvania.

He served as a delegate to the Second Continental Congress, then travelled to France to seek military and financial aid for the warring colonies. Franklin was also one of the diplomats chosen to negotiate peace with Britain at war's end, and was instrumental in achieving the adoption of the U.S. Constitution.

BENJAMIN FRANKLIN

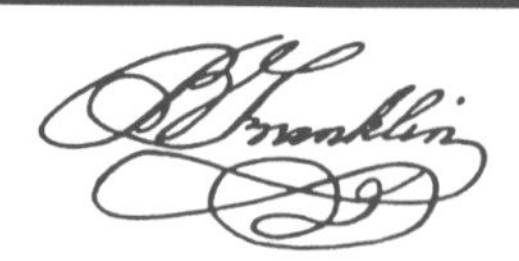

Wise men don't need advice. Fools won't take it.

Beware of little expenses. A small leak will sink a great ship.

The world is full of fools and faint hearts; and yet everyone has courage enough to bear the misfortunes, and wisdom enough to manage the affairs, of his neighbor.

Love your neighbor — but don't pull down your hedge.

Blessed is he that expects nothing, for he shall never be disappointed.

The heart of a fool is in his mouth, but the mouth of a wise man is in his heart.

If passion drives you, let reason hold the reins.

Who is rich? He that rejoices in his portion.

Wealth is not his that has it, but his that enjoys it.

Creditors have better memories than debtors.

The way to see by Faith is to shut the eye of Reason.

He was so learned that he could name a horse in nine languages; so ignorant that he bought a cow to ride on.

If a man could have half his wishes, he would double his troubles.

Love your enemies, for they tell you your faults.

Guests, like fish, begin to smell after three days.

Who is wise? He that learns from everyone. Who is powerful? He that governs his passions. Who is rich? He that is content. Who is that? Nobody.

Teach your child to hold his tongue; he'll learn fast enough to speak.

There are no gains without pains.

B Franklin

Labor leader Lech Walesa became chairman of Solidarity, Communist Poland's first independent trade union. His struggles on behalf of worker's rights have inspired people throughout the world.

Born in Poland in 1943, Walesa attended a state vocational school and began work as an electrician at the Lenin Shipyard in Gdansk. Having witnessed the brutal death of street demonstrators there in 1970, he took up the struggle for truly free trade unions in Poland.

He was elected the head of a strike committee in 1980. Even after the demands of his committee were met, Walesa continued his strike out of solidarity with the other workers in Gdansk.

Solidarity was outlawed after the Polish government imposed martial law, and Walesa was arrested. However, he was awarded the Nobel Peace Prize in 1983. He persisted in his calls for reform despite government harassment, and by 1989 Poland restored legal status to Solidarity.

LECH WALESA

We must be courageous but also reasonable. The world admires us for walking a tightrope without falling off. It asks us to keep our balance.

There will come a time, which I won't see, when narrow Polish problems have been brushed aside, replaced by harmony and peace over our entire planet, and I expect that our children or our children's children will then be able to sing another, more positive song. Until that time we have work to do.

When asked what kind of leader's hat he wears: ''My hat will always be a worker's hat, and it will always hang on a nail. It's a leader's hat but it shall always be a common hat, used by common people for common purposes.''

Everyone wants a voice in human freedom. There's a fire burning inside of all of us.

Confucius was China's most famous teacher, philosopher and political theorist. His ideas have influenced the civilizations of all of eastern Asia.

Confucius was born in 551 B.C. and orphaned at an early age. Although largely self-educated, he became the most learned man of his day. He was disturbed deeply by the social conditions of his time and dedicated his life to social reform. His primary emphasis was on sincerity, and his whole teaching was based upon ethics. He believed that government should make its end not the pleasure of the rulers but the happiness of their subjects.

Unable to obtain an official position in which to effect his ideas of reform, he spent the greater part of his life educating a small group of disciples. His teachings, known as the *Analects,* were compiled by his students after his death. The *Analects* became the basis of the social lifestyle in China — as well as Korea, Japan and Indochina — making Confucius perhaps the most influential man in the world.

C O N F U C I U S

To put the world right in order, we must first put the nation in order; to put the nation in order, we must first put the family in order; to put the family in order, we must first cultivate our personal life; we must first set our hearts right.

Choose a job you love, and you will never have to work a day in your life.

He who is really kind can never be unhappy. He who is really wise can never be confused. He who is really brave is never afraid.

The expectations of life depend upon diligence; the mechanic that would perfect his work must first sharpen his tools.

The superior man is firm in the right way, and not merely firm.

To know what is right and not to do it is the worst cowardice.

Acquire new knowledge whilst thinking over the old, and you may become a teacher of others.

When prosperity comes, do not use all of it.

He who wishes to secure the good of others has already secured his own.

L earning without thought is labor lost.

I t is man that makes truth great, not truth that makes man great.

W ithout knowing the force of words, it is impossible to know more.

O ne joy dispels a hundred cares.

H eaven will be inherited by every man who has heaven in his soul.

W hen you see a worthy person, endeavor to emulate him. When you see an unworthy person, then examine your inner self.

Helen Adams Keller was born in Tuscumbia, Alabama, in 1880. She was deprived of sight, hearing and the ability to speak before the age of two due to a severe illness. Her life represents one of the most extraordinary examples of a person who was able to transcend her physical handicaps.

Through the constant and patient instruction of Anne Sullivan, Helen Keller not only learned to read, write and speak, but went on to graduate *cum laude* from Radcliffe College in 1904.

As well as becoming the author of several articles, books and biographies, she was active on the staffs of the American Foundation for the Blind and the American Foundation for the Overseas Blind. She also lectured in more than 25 countries and received several awards of great distinction.

Helen Keller's courage, faith and optimism in the face of such overwhelming disabilities had a profound effect on all she touched. Her tremendous accomplishments stand as a symbol of the potential in all of us.

HELEN KELLER

Helen Keller

Security is mostly a superstition. It does not exist in nature, nor do the children of men as a whole experience it. Avoiding danger is no safer in the long run than outright exposure. Life is either a daring adventure or nothing.

It gives me a deep, comforting sense that things seen are temporal and things unseen are eternal.

I thank God for my handicaps, for through them, I have found myself, my work, and my God.

Toleration...is the greatest gift of the mind; it requires that same effort of the brain that it takes to balance oneself on a bicycle.

Keep your face to the sunshine and you cannot see the shadows.

Helen Keller

The 33rd President of the United States, Harry S. Truman, faced the tumultuous years at the close of World War II with the blend of honesty, grit and determination that would make him a modern folk hero.

After serving as a captain in World War I, he became a judge and senator before becoming Vice President. When Franklin D. Roosevelt died in 1945, Truman suddenly was faced with some of the most difficult decisions in U.S. history. In swift order he made final arrangements for the charter-writing meeting of the United Nations, helped arrange Germany's unconditional surrender, attended a summit meeting at Potsdam, and brought an end to the war in the Pacific by using the atomic bomb on Hiroshima and Nagasaki.

Elected in his own right in 1948, he went on to implement the Marshall Plan for economic recovery in western Europe and to form the North Atlantic Treaty Organization (NATO) pact, a collective security agreement with non-Communist European nations.

HARRY S. TRUMAN

Harry Truman

We must build a new world, a far better world — one in which the eternal dignity of man is respected.

Study men, not historians.

Men make history and not the other way 'round.

Justice remains the greatest power on earth. To that tremendous power alone will we submit.

Being too good is apt to be uninteresting.

I always considered statesmen to be more expendable than soldiers.

We must have strong minds, ready to accept facts as they are.

Being a President is like riding a tiger. A man has to keep on riding or he is swallowed.

If you can't stand the heat, get out of the kitchen.

A politician is a man who understands government and it takes a politician to run a government. A statesman is a politician who's been dead for fifteen years.

If you can't convince them, confuse them.

Harry Truman

Some of the Presidents were great and some of them weren't. I can say that, because I wasn't one of the great Presidents, but I had a good time trying to be one, I can tell you that.

I have found the best way to give advice to your children is to find out what they want and then advise them to do it.

It's a recession when your neighbor loses his job; it's a depression when you lose your own.

The buck stops here.

It is understanding that gives us an ability to have peace. When we understand the other fellow's viewpoint, and he understands ours, then we can sit down and work out our differences.

Harry Truman

Walt Disney, the pioneer of animated cartoon films, displayed his creative talents at an early age. His interest in art led him to study cartooning through a correspondence school, and he later took classes at the Kansas City Art Institute and School of Design.

In the late 1920s, Disney recognized the potential for sound in cartoon films. He produced "Steamboat Willie," a cartoon short equipped with voices and music, and the character of Mickey Mouse was introduced to the public.

During the economic hard times of the 1930s, Disney's cartoons captivated his audiences. His body of work firmly established him as the unparalleled master of feature-length animated films.

Walt Disney was the recipient of 48 Academy Awards and 7 Emmys. His creativity, ingenuity and ability to bring his fantasies to fruition continue to enchant all ages.

W A L T   D I S N E Y

Walt Disney

It seems to me shallow and arrogant for any man in these times to claim he is completely self-made, that he owes all his success to his own unaided efforts. Many hands and hearts and minds generally contribute to anyone's notable achievements.

Get a good idea and stay with it. Dog it, and work at it until it's done, and done right.

There is great comfort and inspiration in the feeling of close human relationships and its bearing on our mutual fortunes — a powerful force, to overcome the ''tough breaks'' which are certain to come to most of us from time to time.

All our dreams can come true — if we have the courage to pursue them.

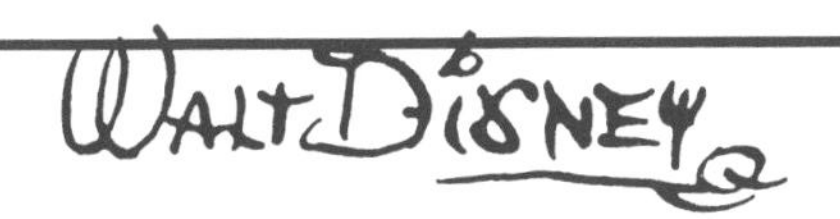

American general, commander-in-chief of the colonial armies in the American Revolution and subsequently the first President of the United States, George Washington became known as the father of his country.

Born into a wealthy family of Virginia planters, Washington worked as a surveyor and gained military experience in the French and Indian War. The impending American Revolution would call him to his country's aid.

Washington was named commander-in-chief of the military force of all the colonies in 1775. Over the next five years, including the nadir of the harsh winter at Valley Forge, Washington held the American forces together by sheer strength of character. His capture of Cornwallis at Yorktown in 1781 marked the end of the war.

Alone commanding the respect of both parties, Washington was chosen unanimously to preside over the Constitutional Convention. He was elected the country's first President in 1789 and re-elected four years later.

GEORGE WASHINGTON

Associate yourself with men of good quality if you esteem your own reputation, for 'tis better to be alone than in bad company.

Few men have virtue to withstand the highest bidder.

True friendship is a plant of slow growth, and must undergo and withstand the shocks of adversity before it is entitled to the appellation.

I hope I shall always possess firmness and virtue enough to maintain what I consider the most enviable of all titles, the character of an honest man.

Liberty, when it begins to take root, is a plant of rapid growth.

G. Washington

Reason, too late perhaps, may convince you of the folly of misspending time.

A slender acquaintance with the world must convince every man that actions, not words, are the true criterion of the attachment of friends.

To be prepared for war is one of the most effectual means of preserving peace.

The time is near at hand which must determine whether Americans are to be free men or slaves.

If the freedom of speech is taken away then dumb and silent we may be led, like sheep to the slaughter.

G. Washington

The basis of our political system is the right of the people to make and to alter their constitution of government.

If, to please the people, we offer what we ourselves disapprove, how can we afterward defend our work? Let us raise a standard to which the wise and honest can repair.

Let your heart feel for the afflictions and distresses of everyone, and let your hand give in proportion to your purse.

Strive not with your superiors in argument, but always submit your judgment to others with modesty.

Last words December 14, 1799: "It is well, I die hard, but I am not afraid to go."

G. Washington

Aristotle, the ancient Greek thinker, philosopher, scientist and writer was one of the greatest minds in ancient times. His contributions to the development of philosophical and scientific systems set the standard for Western intellectual thinking.

His importance to the scientific world is unparalleled. Aristotle invented the study of formal logic and applied its principles to physics, chemistry, biology and zoology. Also, his ability to look at the phenomenon of human existence stretched across the areas of psychology and literature. Aristotle's writings and oratory on political and ethical theory still are read and debated in modern-day philosophy.

A R I S T O T L E

The difference between an educated and uneducated man is the same difference as between being alive and being dead.

Hope is a waking dream.

Beauty is the gift of God.

What is a friend? A single soul dwelling in two bodies.

Education is the best provision for old age.

We should behave to our friends as we would wish our friends to behave to us.

In all things of nature there is something of the marvelous.

The actuality of thought is life.

For the things we have to learn before we can do them, we learn by doing them.

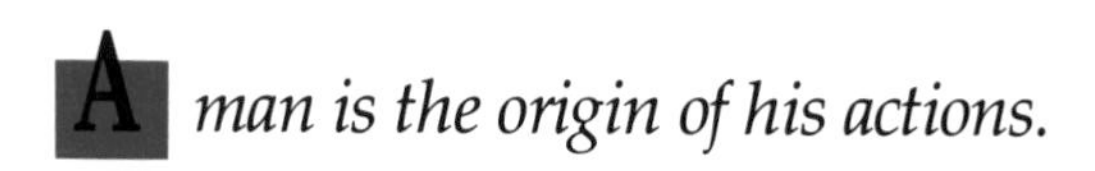

A man is the origin of his actions.

Without friends no one would choose to live, though he had all other goods.

Nature does nothing uselessly.

Well begun is half done.

Misfortune shows those who are not really friends.

A likely impossibility is always preferable to an unconvincing possibility.

With regard to excellence, it is not enough to know, but we must try to have and use it.

Dignity consists not in possessing honors, but in the consciousness that we deserve them.

Men acquire a particular quality by constantly acting in a particular way.

The end of labor is to gain leisure.

It is better to rise from life as from a banquet — neither thirsty nor drunken.

The 32nd President of the United States, Franklin Delano Roosevelt, served for more than 12 years, longer than any other man. He greatly expanded federal powers to effect economic recovery during the Great Depression and was a major Allied leader during World War II.

Roosevelt attended Harvard University and the Columbia University School of Law. He was elected to the New York Senate in 1910 and became assistant secretary of the Navy three years later. He remained active in Democratic politics despite being stricken by polio and was elected governor of New York in 1928.

Elected President in 1931, Roosevelt quickly obtained passage of a sweeping economic program, the New Deal, which provided relief, loans and jobs through a variety of federal agencies. Roosevelt mobilized industry for military production and extended aid to Great Britain. He played a leading role in creating the alliance with Britain and the U.S.S.R. that led to victory in World War II.

FRANKLIN D. ROOSEVELT

When you come to the end of your rope, tie a knot and hang on.

Let me assert my firm belief that the only thing we have to fear is fear itself.

We look forward to a world founded upon four essential human freedoms. The first is freedom of speech and expression. The second is freedom of every person to worship God in his own way. The third is freedom from want....The fourth is freedom from fear.

We have always held to the hope, the belief, the conviction that there is a better life, a better world, beyond the horizon.

The only limit to our realization of tomorrow will be our doubts of today.

Franklin D Roosevelt

The truth is found when men are free to pursue it.

On speech-making: ''Be sincere; be brief; be seated.''

Happiness lies in the joy of achievement and the thrill of creative effort.

There is no indispensable man.

The test of our progress is not whether we add more to the abundance of those who have much; it is whether we provide enough for those who have too little.

Franklin D. Roosevelt

The future lies with those wise political leaders who realize that the great public is interested more in government than in politics.

We, and all others who believe in freedom as deeply as we do, would rather die on our feet than live on our knees.

The nation that destroys its soil destroys itself.

The ablest man I ever met is the man you think you are.

More than an end to war, we want an end to the beginnings of all wars.

Franklin D Roosevelt

Margaret Thatcher is the first woman in European history to be elected prime minister.

The daughter of a grocer, she received her degree in chemistry at Oxford, where she became president of the University Conservative Association. During the 1950's, she worked as a research chemist and also studied law, specializing in taxation.

She first ran for Parliament in 1950, but it was not until 1959 that she was finally elected to the House of Commons. She served as parliamentary secretary to the Ministry of Pensions and National Insurance, and later as secretary of state for education and science.

Thatcher was elected the leader of the Conservative Party in 1975, and the party's victory in the 1979 elections elevated her to the office of prime minister.

MARGARET THATCHER

You may have to fight a battle more than once to win it.

What is success? I think it is a mixture of having a flair for the thing that you are doing; knowing that it is not enough, that you have got to have hard work and a certain sense of purpose.

Let our children grow tall and some taller than others if they have it in them to do so.

I am not hard — I'm frightfully soft. But I will not be hounded.

U-turn if you want to. This lady's not for turning.

Margaret H. Thatcher

Victorian values. . .were the values when our country became great.

I wasn't lucky. I deserved it.

Speaking on diplomacy: ''You don't tell deliberate lies, but sometimes you have to be evasive.''

To wear your heart on your sleeve isn't a very good plan; you should wear it inside, where it functions best.

I do not know anyone who has got or gotten to the top without hard work. That is the recipe.

Margaret H. Thatcher

I'm extraordinarily patient provided I get my own way in the end.

I don't mind how much my ministers talk — as long as they do what I say.

I usually make up my mind about a man in ten seconds, and I very rarely change it.

Being powerful is like being a lady. If you have to tell people you are, you aren't.

Pennies do not come from heaven. They have to be earned here on earth.

Born in a log cabin in the wilds of the Carolinas and orphaned at the age of 14, Andrew Jackson grew up with the frontier spirit of one always ready to defend honor and country. His self-reliance and determination would serve him well as a lawyer, judge, congressman, senator, military hero and the seventh President of the United States.

It was his heroism in the War of 1812 that earned him the nickname "Old Hickory" and thrust him into national prominence. Jackson and his Tennessee militia defeated the British at New Orleans, marking the end of the fighting.

His military triumphs led to his nomination as President, and he was elected in 1828. His election marked the first time a President was elected from the area west of Appalachians and the first time an election focused on direct mass appeal to the voters. This rising tide of democratic sentiment became known as "Jacksonian Democracy."

ANDREW JACKSON

Andrew Jackson

One man with courage makes a majority.

The brave man inattentive to his duty is worth little more to his country than the coward who deserts in the hour of danger.

Peace, above all things, is to be desired, but blood must sometimes be spilled to obtain it on equitable and lasting terms.

You must pay the price if you wish to secure the blessings.

Every good citizen makes his country's honor his own and cherishes it not only as precious but as sacred. He is willing to risk his life in its defense and is conscious that he gains protection while he gives it.

Andrew Jackson

Leader of the Indian Nationalist movement against British rule, Mohandas "Mahatma" Gandhi is revered as the father of his country. He is esteemed internationally for his doctrine of nonviolence to achieve political and social progress.

Gandhi received an education in India before beginning law studies in England in 1888. Seeking clerical work in South Africa, he was shocked at the racial discrimination he encountered. He became an advocate for his fellow Indians, and his challenges to the government resulted in a jail sentence.

He entered politics in India in 1919 to protest British sedition laws. He emerged as the head of the Indian National Congress, where he advocated a policy of nonviolent protest to achieve Indian independence. Repressed throughout World War II, Gandhi successfully negotiated for an autonomous Indian state in 1947. He was assassinated one year later.

MAHATMA GANDHI

M K Gandhi

The weak can never forgive. Forgiveness is the attribute of the strong.

Hatred can be overcome only by love.

Truth resides in every human heart, and one has to search for it there and to be guided by truth as one sees it. But no one has a right to coerce others to act according to his own view of truth.

Freedom is not worth having if it does not connote freedom to err.

There is no god higher than truth.

M K Gandhi

Patience means self-suffering.

Cowards can never be moral.

Satisfaction lies in the effort, not in the attainment. Full effort is full victory.

Where there is love there is life.

Let us fear God and we shall cease to fear man.

No culture can live if it attempts to be exclusive.

M K Gandhi

F *aith...must be enforced by reason ....When faith becomes blind it dies.*

U *nity to be real must stand the severest strain without breaking.*

T *he only tyrant I accept in this world is the still voice within.*

H *onest differences are often a healthy sign of progress.*

A *"no" uttered from the deepest conviction is better and greater than a "yes" merely uttered to please, or what is worse, to avoid trouble.*

M.K. Gandhi

John F. Kennedy was elected the 35th president of the United States at the age of 43 — the youngest man and first Roman Catholic ever elected.

Kennedy graduated from Harvard University in 1936 and joined the U.S. Navy shortly before World War II. While on active duty in the Pacific, the Japanese destroyed the boat under his command, PT 109. Despite a back injury, Kennedy showed great heroism in rescuing his crew.

After holding seats in both the House and Senate, Kennedy was elected president in 1960. His style, charisma and oratory won him admiration at home and abroad, but his life was tragically cut short by an assasin's bullet in 1963. His major accomplishments include the formation of the Peace Corps and his deft handling of the Cuban Missile Crisis. His book, *Profiles in Courage,* won the Pulitzer Prize in 1957.

JOHN F. KENNEDY

And so, my fellow Americans, ask not what your country can do for you, ask what you can do for your country.

We must seek, above all, a world of peace; a world in which peoples dwell together in mutual respect and work together in mutual regard.

The energy, the faith, the devotion which we bring to this endeavor will light our country and all who serve it, and the glow from that fire can truly light the world.

Those who make peaceful revolution impossible will make violent revolution inevitable.

The time to repair the roof is when the sun is shining.

Happiness is the full use of your powers along lines of excellence in a life affording scope.

I look forward to . . . a future in which our country will match its military strength with our moral restraint, its wealth with our wisdom, its power with our purpose.

A man does what he must — in spite of personal consequences, in spite of obstacles and dangers and pressures — and that is the basis of all human morality.

A child miseducated is a child lost.

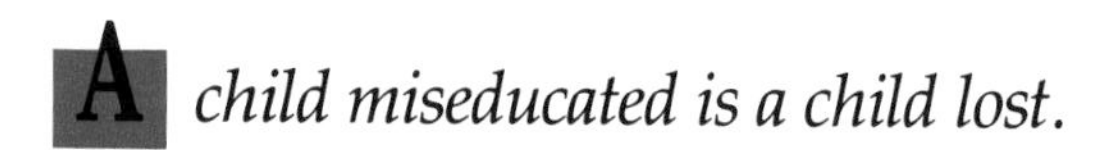

Forgive your enemies, but never forget their names.

When power leads man toward arrogance, poetry reminds him of his limitations. When power narrows the area of man's concern, poetry reminds him of the richness and diversity of existence. When power corrupts, poetry cleanses.

For of those to whom much is given, much is required.

For without belittling the courage with which men have died, we should not forget those acts of courage with which men have lived.

Let us never negotiate out of fear but let us never fear to negotiate.

One of the greatest scientific minds of all time, Albert Einstein is best known for his contributions to the field of physics. Born in Germany in 1879, Einstein received his diploma from the Swiss Federal Polytechnic School in Zurich, where he trained as a teacher in physics and mathematics. In 1905, he received his Ph.D. and published four research papers, the most significant being the creation of the special theory of relativity. He became internationally famous when he was awarded the Nobel Prize for Physics in 1922.

The important military implications of the discovery of the fission of uranium in 1939 led Einstein to appeal to President Franklin Roosevelt. Einstein's letter to the president led to the development of the atomic bomb.

Einstein left the field of physics greatly changed through his brilliant contributions. His discoveries provided the impetus for future research into understanding the mysteries of the universe.

ALBERT EINSTEIN

Albert Einstein.

Try not to become a man of success but rather try to become a man of value.

A hundred times a day I remind myself that my life depends on the labors of other men, living and dead, and that I must exert myself in order to give, in the measure as I have received, and am still receiving.

The high destiny of the individual is to serve rather than to rule.

In the middle of difficulty lies opportunity.

When I examine myself and my methods of thought, I come to the conclusion that the gift of fantasy has meant more to me than my talent for absorbing positive knowledge.

Albert Einstein.

Anger dwells only in the bosom of fools.

He who can no longer pause to wonder and stand rapt in awe is as good as dead; his eyes are closed.

An empty stomach is not a good political advisor.

I never think of the future. It comes soon enough.

When a man sits with a pretty girl for an hour, it seems like a minute. But let him sit on a hot stove for a minute — and it's longer than any hour. That's relativity.

I think and think for months and years. Ninety-nine times, the conclusion is false. The hundredth time I am right.

Albert Einstein.

Solitude is painful when one is young, but delightful when one is more mature.

The most beautiful thing we can experience is the mysterious. It is the source of all true art and science.

The whole of science is nothing more than a refinement of everyday thinking.

Everything should be made as simple as possible, but not simpler.

The important thing is not to stop questioning. Curiosity has its own reason for existing. One cannot help but be in awe when he contemplates the mysteries of eternity, of life, of the marvelous structure of reality. It is enough if one tries merely to comprehend a little of this mystery every day. Never lose a holy curiosity.

Albert Einstein.

Woodrow Wilson already had excelled as a scholar, teacher and the President of Princeton University before launching a career in politics that would lead him to his country's highest office.

He served as the governor of New Jersey before becoming President in 1912. In his first term, he remarkably was able to carry through legislation, including the Federal Reserve Act and the formation of the Federal Trade Commission. His second term brought the United States into World War I.

The depth of his idealistic fervor gave force to his political leadership, and U.S. intervention soon brought the war to an end. His Fourteen Points became the basis for the German peace. He was instrumental in forming the League of Nations and concluding the Versailles Treaty. He was awarded the Nobel Prize for Peace in 1919.

WOODROW WILSON

Woodrow Wilson

It must be peace without victory. . .Only a peace between equals can last.

A conservative is a man who just sits and thinks, mostly sits.

He is more apt to contribute heat than light to a discussion.

Conservatism is the policy of make no change and consult your grandmother when in doubt.

Golf is an ineffectual attempt to put an elusive ball into an obscure hole with implements ill-adapted to the purpose.

Woodrow Wilson

A Yankee always thinks that he is right; a Scotch-Irishman knows that he is right.

Sometimes people call me an idealist. Well, that is the way I know I am an American. America is the only idealistic nation in the world.

Right is more precious than peace.

Business underlies everything in our national life, including our spiritual life.

No one can worship God or love his neighbor on an empty stomach.

Woodrow Wilson

America lives in the heart of every man everywhere who wishes to find a region.

Interest does not tie nations together, it sometimes separates them. But sympathy and understanding do unite them.

Liberty has never come from the government. Liberty has always come from the subjects of it. The history of liberty is a history of resistance.

No nation is fit to set in judgment upon any other nation.

Woodrow Wilson

Soldier, writer, statesman, Charles de Gaulle rose to world fame as the symbol of French resistance during World War II. He became the founding president of France's Fifth Republic, and served from 1958 to 1969.

A lieutenant in World War I, de Gaulle was three times wounded and spent three years as a prisoner of war. When World War II broke out, de Gaulle was promoted to Undersecretary of War. With the rise of the pro-German Vichy Government, de Gaulle fled to England. His radio appeals to the French people to resist and continue the struggle earned him a death sentence *in absentia.* However, de Gaulle persisted in building up the Free French and resistance forces.

Ultimately, he received the support of the Allied leaders and became president of the provisional government in 1944. In 1958, de Gaulle was again called upon to form a new government, and became president of the Fifth Republic.

CHARLES DE GAULLE

C. de Gaulle

Nothing great will ever be achieved without great men, and men are great only if they are determined to be so.

History does not teach fatalism. These are moments when the will of a handful of free men breaks through determinism and opens up new roads. People get the history they deserve.

The graveyards are full of indispensable men.

For glory gives herself only to those who have always dreamed of her.

How can one conceive of a one-party system in a country that has over two hundred varieties of cheese?

C. de Gaulle

Since a politician never believes what he says, he is surprised when others believe him.

Treaties are like roses and young girls — they last while they last.

Deliberation is the work of many men. Action, of one alone.

I have come to the conclusion that politics is too serious a matter to be left to the politicians.

I respect those who resist me, but I cannot tolerate them.

C. de Gaulle

Silence is the ultimate weapon of power.

To govern is always to choose among disadvantages.

The great leaders have always stage-managed their effects.

Diplomats are useful only in fair weather. As soon as it rains they drown in every drop.

Every man of action has a strong dose of egoism, pride, hardness, and cunning. But all those things will be regarded as high qualities if he can make them the means to achieve great ends.

C. de Gaulle

Mother Teresa, born Agnes Gonxha Bojarhiu, is revered for her lifelong dedication to the poor, most notably the destitute masses of India.

In 1928, at the age of 18, she went to Ireland to join the Institute of the Blessed Virgin Mary and shortly thereafter traveled to India to work with the poor of Calcutta. After studying nursing, she moved into the slums of the city where she founded the Order of the Missionaries of Charity. Mother Teresa was summoned to Rome in 1968 to found a home for the needy, and three years later she was awarded the first Pope John XXIII Peace Prize.

By the late 1970s, the Missionaries of Charity numbered more than 1,000 nuns who operated 60 centers in Calcutta and more than 200 centers worldwide. Her selfless commitment to helping the poor saved the lives of nearly 8,000 people in Calcutta alone. Mother Teresa's compassion and devotion to the destitute earned her the Nobel Peace Prize in 1979.

M O T H E R   T E R E S A

We can do no great things — only small things with great love.

I am a little pencil in the hand of a writing God who is sending a love letter to the world.

The biggest disease today is not leprosy or tuberculosis, but rather the feeling of being unwanted.

Many people mistake our work for our vocation. Our vocation is the love of Jesus.

I do not pray for success. I ask for faithfulness.

Loneliness and the feeling of being unwanted is the most terrible poverty.

Dale Carnegie was a pioneer in public speaking and personality development. He became famous by showing others how to become successful. His book *How to Win Friends and Influence People* has sold more than 10 million copies and has been translated into more than 30 languages.

His teachings became popular because of his illustrative stories and simple, well-phrased rules. Toward the beginning of his career, Carnegie wrote *Public Speaking and Influencing Men in Business,* which became the standard text for public-speaking courses.

Dale Carnegie organized his works into a series of lectures led by his students. The teachings of the Carnegie Institute for Effective Speaking and Human Relations have been the cornerstone of many successful business careers over the past 50 years. Dale Carnegie was living proof of his message that success is the result of persistence, patience and personal initiative.

DALE CARNEGIE

Dale Carnegie

The ideas I stand for are not mine. I borrowed them from Socrates. I swiped them from Chesterfield. I stole them from Jesus. And I put them in a book. If you don't like their rules, whose would you use?

The man who goes farthest is generally the one who is willing to do and dare. The sure-thing boat never gets far from the shore.

You can make more friends in two months by becoming interested in other people than you can in two years by trying to get other people interested in you.

Flattery is from the teeth out. Sincere appreciation is from the heart out.

When dealing with people, remember you are not dealing with creatures of logic, but with creatures of emotion.

Dale Carnegie

First ask yourself: What is the worst that can happen? Then prepare to accept it. Then proceed to improve on the worst.

You never achieve real success unless you like what you are doing.

If you want to gather honey, don't kick over the beehive.

If only the people who worry about their liabilities would think about the riches they do possess, they would stop worrying.

Add up what you have, and you'll find that you won't sell them for all the gold in the world.

Dale Carnegie

The best things in life are yours, if you can appreciate yourself.

Develop success from failures. Discouragement and failure are two of the surest stepping stones to success.

When you're afraid, keep your mind on what you have to do. . . . if you have been thoroughly prepared, you will not be afraid.

The successful man will profit from his mistakes and try again in a different way.

We all have possibilities we don't know about. We can do things we don't even dream we can do.

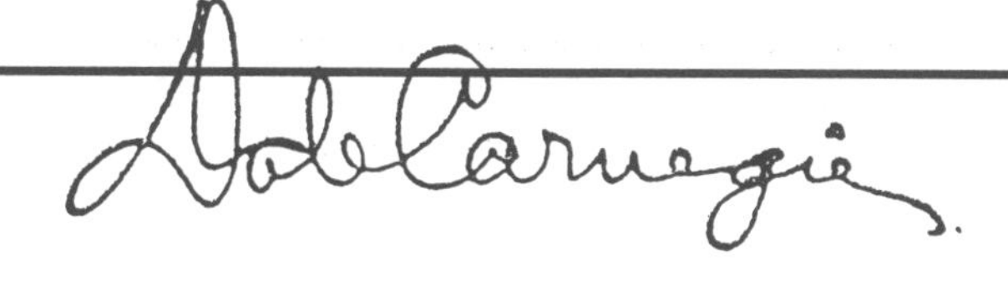

Douglas MacArthur graduated from West Point with the highest honors in his class. Brilliant and controversial, he carried his ambition and lust for achievement through posts in World War I, World War II, and the Korean War.

During the course of World War I, MacArthur was promoted to full general and became army chief of staff. MacArthur battled the Japanese in the Phillipines during World War II, and served as Allied commander of the Japanese occupation.

The Korean War began in 1950, and MacArthur was soon selected to command United Nations forces there. After initial success, he then encountered massive Chinese resistance and entered into a bitter dispute with President Truman. Despite Truman's insistence on a limited war, MacArthur persisted in initiating the offensive. He was relieved of command by Truman for insubordination in 1951. Ever aloof and enigmatic, MacArthur retired to private life, the symbol of zealous dedication to duty, honor and country.

DOUGLAS MAC ARTHUR

Douglas MacArthur

Youth is not entirely a time of life; it is a state of mind. Nobody grows old by merely living a number of years. People grow old by deserting their ideals. You are as young as your faith, as old as your doubt; as young as your self-confidence, as old as your fear; as young as your hope, as old as your despair.

There is no security in this life, only opportunity.

Only those are fit to live who are not afraid to die.

It is fatal to enter any war without the will to win it.

Douglas MacArthur

Duty, honor, country: Those three hallowed words reverently dictate what you ought to be, what you can be, what you will be.

I would hope that our beloved country will drink deep from the chalice of courage.

In war, you win or lose, live or die — and the difference is just an eyelash.

Upon the fields of friendly strife are sown the seeds that, upon other fields, on other days, will bear the fruits of victory.

In war there is no substitute for victory.

Douglas MacArthur

Build me a son, O Lord, who will be strong enough to know when he is weak, and brave enough to face himself when he is afraid, one who will be proud and unbending in honest defeat, and humble and gentle in victory.

In the central place of every heart there is a recording chamber. So long as it receives a message of beauty, hope, cheer, and courage — so long are you young. When the wires are all down and our heart is covered with the snow of pessimism and the ice of cynicism, then, and only the, are you grown old.

And in the end, through the long ages of our quest for light, it will be found that truth is still mightier than the sword.

Douglas MacArthur

A keen student of the game and a master motivator, John Wooden was one of the greatest coaches in college basketball history. He led his teams at the University of California at Los Angeles to a record 10 NCAA championships.

As a player at Purdue University, Wooden earned All-America honors in 1930, 1931 and 1932. He coached high school basketball before serving in the U.S. Navy during World War II. After the war, he became head basketball coach and athletic director at Indiana State Teachers' College. He was appointed head coach at UCLA in 1948.

At UCLA, he parlayed the talents of such stars as Lew Alcindor (later Kareem Abdul-Jabbar), Gail Goodrich and Bill Walton into a virtual college basketball dynasty. His teams won a record seven straight NCAA championships from 1967-1973. From 1971 to 1974, UCLA won 88 consecutive games, a college basketball record. John Wooden is the only person named to the Basketball Hall of Fame as both a player and a coach.

JOHN WOODEN

John Wooden

Ability may get you to the top, but it takes character to keep you there.

Do not let what you cannot do interfere with what you can do.

Don't measure yourself by what you have accomplished, but by what you should have accomplished with your ability.

Failure to prepare is preparing to fail.

Be more concerned with your character than with your reputation. Your character is what you really are while your reputation is merely what others think you are.

Success is peace of mind in knowing you did your best.

John Wooden

Celebrated as both a technological genius and a folk hero, Henry Ford was the creative force in the automotive industry. His innovations changed the economic and social character of his country — and the world.

Ford developed the mass-produced "Model T" automobile and sold it at a price the average person could afford. Use of the assembly line in mass production saved time and money and allowed Ford to offer more cars to the American public at a lower price than anyone before him. More than 15 million "Model T's" were sold in the United States between 1908 and 1927.

A noted philanthropist, Ford established Greenfield Village, a group of historical buildings and landmarks in Dearborn, Michigan. He also established the Henry Ford Museum and the Ford Foundation.

HENRY FORD

Henry Ford

Anyone who stops learning is old, whether at twenty or eighty. Anyone who keeps learning stays young. The greatest thing in life is to keep your mind young.

Failure is only the opportunity to begin again more intelligently.

Whether you think you can or think you can't — you are right.

Coming together is a beginning; keeping together is progress; working together is success.

Nothing is particularly hard if you divide it into small jobs.

Henry Ford

If money is your hope for independence you will never have it. The only real security that a man can have in this world is a reserve of knowledge, experience and ability.

The high wage begins down in the shop. If it is not created there it cannot get into pay envelopes. There will never be a system invented which will do away with necessity for work.

My best friend is the one who brings out the best in me.

It is not the employer who pays wages — he only handles the money. It is the product that pays wages.

Even a mistake may turn out to be the one thing necessary to a worthwhile achievement.

Henry Ford

Business is never so healthy as when, like a chicken, it must do a certain amount of scratching for what it gets.

A bore is a fellow who opens his mouth and puts his feats in it.

Don't find fault. Find a remedy.

An idealist is a person who helps other people to be prosperous.

There is joy in work.... There is no happiness except in the realization that we have accomplished something.

Henry Ford

Born into slavery in 1856, Booker T. Washington went on to become the most influential black leader and educator of his time. He believed that blacks could benefit more from a practical, vocational education than a college education. His work toward economic prosperity for blacks led to his role as founder and head of Tuskegee Institute, a vocational school for blacks in Tuskegee, Alabama.

The success of Tuskegee Institute as well as Washington's strong belief in mutual progress of blacks and whites made him a shrewd political leader — and an advisor to presidents, congressmen and governors. His autobiography, *Up From Slavery,* was a best-seller that described his rise to national prominence.

In a period of escalating racial tension, Washington's supportive approach was popular with blacks and whites alike. This period became justly known as the "Age of Booker T. Washington."

BOOKER T. WASHINGTON

Booker T. Washington.

I have learned that success is to be measured not so much by the position that one has reached in life as by the obstacles which one has overcome while trying to succeed.

You can't hold a man down without staying down with him.

No race can prosper 'til it learns that there is as much dignity in tilling a field as in writing a poem.

The world cares very little about what a man or woman knows; it is what the man or woman is able to do that counts.

Excellence is to do a common thing in an uncommon way.

Booker T. Washington.

Legendary Alabama football coach Bear Bryant was a strict disciplinarian and the model of integrity and fairness. His remarkable overall career record stands at 323 wins, 85 losses and 17 ties.

Growing up in Fordyce, Arkansas, Paul Bryant earned his famous nickname wrestling a bear for money at a sideshow attraction. At Fordyce High School, he was an all-state lineman on the state championship football team of 1930. He went on to play at the University of Alabama before beginning his coaching career.

Bryant held head coaching jobs at the University of Maryland, the University of Kentucky and Texas Argricultural and Mechanical University before returning to coach Alabama in 1958. Six of his Alabama teams were ranked first nationally, and they played in 24 straight bowl games. Bryant was named National Coach of the Year in 1961, 1971 and 1973, and was elected to the College Football Hall of Fame in his first year of eligibility.

PAUL BEAR BRYANT

Paul "Bear" Bryant

My attitude has always been...if it's worth playing, it's worth paying the price to win.

On the three types of individuals who play the game: "First, there are those who are winners and know they are winners. Then there are the losers who know they are losers. Then there are those who are not winners but don't know it. They're the ones for me. They never quit trying. They're the soul of our game."

In order to have a winner, the team must have a feeling of unity; every player must put the team first — ahead of personal glory.

When asked if he walked on water: "Well, I won't say I can or I can't; but if I do, I do it before most people get up in the morning."

Paul "Bear" Bryant

They say I teach brutal football, but the only thing brutal about football is losing.

Most coaches study the films when they lose. I study them when we win — to see if I can figure out what I did right.

I've never recommended anybody go into coaching, 'cause if they have enough on the ball, if they can do without coaching, they should do without it. If they put as much work into it and spend as much time, the rewards are going to be much better in something else.

I ain't never had much fun. I ain't never been two inches away from a football. Here guys go fishing on the day of the game, hunting, golfing, and all I want to do is be alone, studying how not to lose.

Paul "Bear" Bryant

I ain't won but one. My team won the rest in spite of me.

Football games are generally won by the boys with the greatest desire.

Justifying the role of athletics: ''It's kind of hard to rally 'round a math class.''

I knew it was time to leave when they had a banquet and they gave Aldolph a Cadillac and gave me a cigarette lighter.

When asked what he most wanted to be remembered for: ''I'd like if it'd be for winning. . .''

Paul "Bear" Bryant

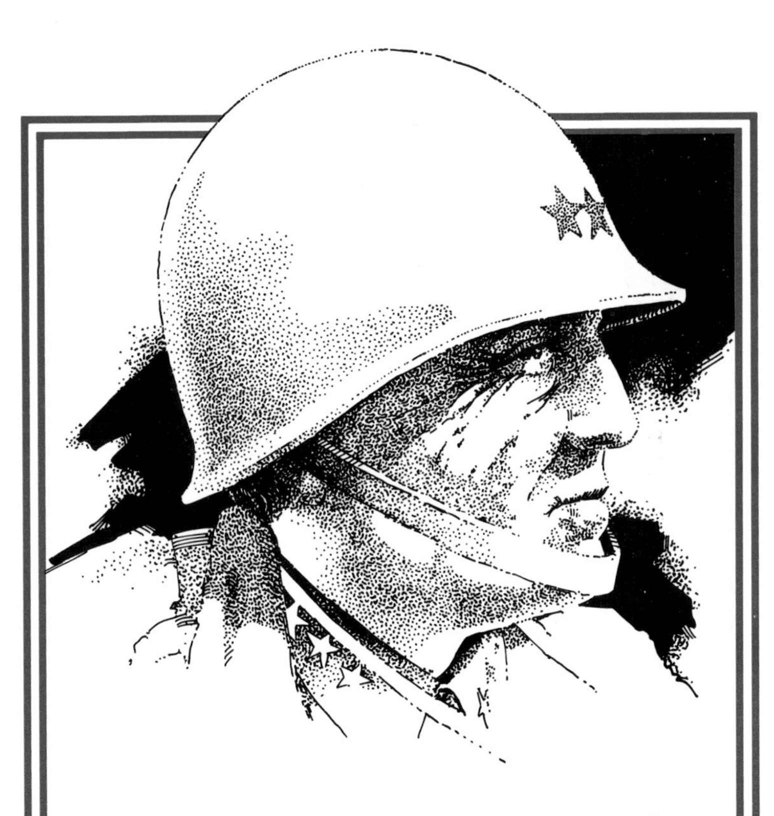

Relentless, hard-driving and tenacious are only a few adjectives to describe George S. Patton Jr., one of the foremost American combat generals of World War II. He was the chief proponent of the adoption of mobile weapons and armored vehicles, and his bravery as a tank commander played a major role in halting the German counterattack at the Battle of the Bulge.

His ruthless sweep across France in the summer of 1944 defied conventional military wisdom, but culminated in spectacular success. By January 1945, Patton's forces had reached the German border, capturing thousands of German troops.

Patton was one of the most colorful and controversial figures in military history. Although his outspoken comments and unpredictable actions often were criticized by civilian authorities, he instilled exceptional pride in his men. His toughness earned him the nickname "Old Blood-and-Guts."

GEORGE S. PATTON, JR.

G S Patton Jr.

If everyone is thinking alike then somebody isn't thinking.

Accept the challenges so that you may feel the exhilaration of victory.

Wars may be fought with weapons, but they are won by men. It is the spirit of the men who follow and of the man who leads that gains the victory.

The most vital quality a soldier can possess is self-confidence.

Never tell people how to do things. Tell them what to do and they will surprise you with their ingenuity.

G. S. Patton Jr.

Y ou must be single minded. Drive for the one thing on which you have decided.

A lways do more than is required of you.

N ow if you are going to win any battle you have to do one thing. You have to make the mind run the body. Never let the body tell the mind what to do.

T he fixed determination to acquire the warrior soul, and to have acquired it to either conquer or perish with honor, is the secret of victory.

A civil servant is sometimes like a broken cannon — it won't work and you can't fire it.

G S Patton Jr.

For years I have been accused of making snap judgments. Honestly, this is not the case because I am a profound military student and thoughts I express, perhaps too flippantly, are the result of years of thought and study.

I do not fear failure. I only fear the ''slowing up'' of the engine inside of me which is pounding, saying, ''Keep going, someone must be on top, why not you?''

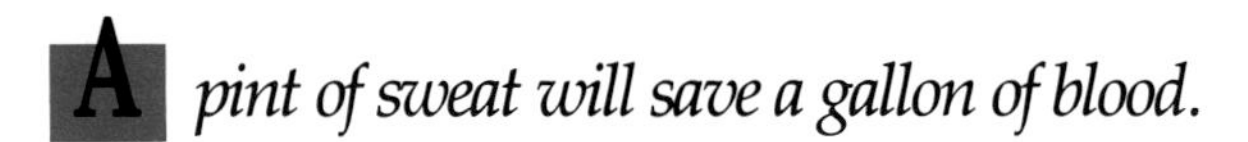

A pint of sweat will save a gallon of blood.

If a man has done his best, what else is there?

G S Patton Jr.

When Pope John Paul II was invested in 1978, he became the first Polish pope in the Church's history — and the first non-Italian pope in 456 years. This remarkable man has encompassed the globe to bring the doctrine of the Catholic Church to the world's people.

Born Karol Wojtyla in Wadowice, Poland, he studied Polish literature and worked in a chemical factory before the outbreak of World War II. Determined to become a priest, he went into hiding at the palace of the archbishop of Krakow and was ordained in 1946. He later became archbishop of Krakow after receiving a doctorate in ethics and becoming a professor of philosophy. He was made cardinal in 1967, and elected pope just over 10 years later.

His fluency in a number of languages uniquely qualifies him as an international ambassador for the Church. His passionate commitment to spread the Word of God has continued unabated, despite an assassination attempt in 1981.

POPE JOHN PAUL II

Joannes Paulus pp II

War should belong to the tragic past, to history: it should find no place on humanity's agenda for the future.

If you wish to be brothers, drop your weapons.

You must strive to multiply bread so that it suffices for the tables of mankind.

When freedom does not have a purpose, when it does not wish to know anything about the rule of law engraved in the hearts of men and women, when it does not listen to the voice of conscience, it turns against humanity and society.

To maintain a joyful family requires much from both the parents and the children. Each member of the family has to become, in a special way, the servant of the others.

Joannes Paulus pp II

It was a blend of honesty, humility and persistence that marked Dwight D. Eisenhower's success as both the 34th President of the United States and as the supreme commander of the Allied forces during World War II.

Eisenhower graduated from West Point and commanded a tank training center during World War I. At the outbreak of World War II, Eisenhower was appointed to the Army's war plans division, where he prepared strategy for the Allied invasion of Europe. He was later selected commander of U.S. troops in Europe.

He retired to become President of Columbia University and publish his best-selling account of the war. Wooed by both parties, Eisenhower ran as a Republican for President in 1952 and 1956, winning both times. Eisenhower enjoyed tremendous popularity with the American people, and worked to expand Social Security and increase the minimum wage. In addition, he created the Department of Health, Education and Welfare and NASA.

DWIGHT D. EISENHOWER

Whatever America hopes to bring to pass in the world must first come to pass in the heart of America.

We have heard much of the phrase, "peace and friendship." This phrase, in expressing the aspiration of America, is not complete. We should say instead, "peace and friendship, in freedom." This, I think, is America's real message to the rest of the world.

An intellectual is a man who takes more words than necessary to tell more than he knows.

Farming looks mighty easy when your plow is a pencil and you're a thousand miles from the corn field.

Only our individual faith in freedom can keep us free.

Dwight D. Eisenhower

Though force can protect in emergency, only justice, fairness, consideration and cooperation can finally lead men to the dawn of eternal peace.

Freedom has its life in the hearts, the actions, the spirit of men and so it must be daily earned and refreshed — else like a flower cut from its life-giving roots, it will wither and die.

Leadership: the art of getting someone else to do something you want done because he wants to do it.

The free world must not prove itself worthy of its own past.

We seek peace, knowing that peace is the climate of freedom.

Dwight D. Eisenhower

I have one yardstick by which I test every major problem — and that yardstick is: Is it good for America?

Neither a wise man nor a brave man lies down on the tracks of history to wait for the train of the future to run over him.

The problem in defense is how far you can go without destroying from within what you are trying to defend from without.

May we pursue that right — without self-righteousness. May we know unity — without conformity. May we grow in strength — without pride of self. May we, in our dealings with all people of the earth, ever speak the truth and serve justice. May the light of freedom, coming to all darkened lands, flame brightly — until at last the darkness is no more.

Other Books by Celebrating Excellence

Great Quotes from Great Women

Great Quotes from Great Leaders

The Best of Success

Never Never Quit

Commitment to Excellence

Management Magic

Motivational Quotes

Customer Care

Opportunity Selling

Commitment to Quality

America: It's People, It's Pride and It's Progress

Zig Ziglar's Favorite Quotations

Think: Creativity and Innovation

Winning With Teamwork

The Power of Goals

Your Attitude Determines Your Altitude

Motivation Lombardi Style

Th. Jefferson
Booker T. Washington
Henry Ford
Paul "Bear" Bryant
Theodore Roosevelt
Harry Truman
Albert Einstein
Th. Jefferson
Dale Carnegie
Theodore Roosevelt
Albert Schweitzer
Vince Lombardi
G. Washington
Martin Luther King, Jr.
Abraham Lincoln
G. S. Patton, Jr.
[illegible]
Harry Truman
Dwight D. Eisenhower
Golda Meir
Dwight D. Eisenhower
Franklin D. Roosevelt
Andrew Jackson
B. Franklin
Paul "Bear" Bryant
Joannes Paulus PP II
Booker T. Washington
Douglas MacArthur
Abraham Lincoln
Douglas MacArthur
M. K. Gandhi
Dwight D. Eisenhower
C. de Gaulle
Walt Disney
Harry Truman
Norman Vincent Peale
Franklin D. Roosevelt
Henry Ford
Helen Keller
G. Washington
Vince Lombardi
Booker T. Washington
John Wooden
M. K. Gandhi
C. de Gaulle
Dale Carnegie
Albert Einstein
Andrew Jackson
Joannes Paulus PP II
Golda Meir
Golda Meir
B. Franklin
[illegible]
Paul "Bear" Bryant
Walt Disney
M. K. Gandhi
Henry Ford
Walt Disney
Dale Carnegie
[illegible]